D,

It may even help!

You love life . .

Merry Christmas

love

Sam

THE *Carluccio's* COLLECTION

VEGETABLES & SALADS

ANTONIO & PRISCILLA CARLUCCIO

Photography by André Martin

ANTONIO CARLUCCIO

QUADRILLE

Contents

All recipes are for 4 unless otherwise stated. Use either
all metric or all imperial measures, as the two are not
necessarily interchangeable.

Foreword

For me, Italian markets are all about bunches of freshly cut *cicorietta* (a slightly bitter and tender salad leaf), masses of courgette flowers, fresh green beans or fresh mint, basil and oregano just picked in the hills, and a couple of dozen warm eggs from corn-fed hens.

The first thing I do when I am in Italy is to go to the local market, quite early in the morning, to meet some of the old women who sit in front of their baskets full of bunches of anything green and edible, neatly tied up with small stalks of fresh willow. Aside from the romance of dealing with women vendors (who are often pretty tough!) there is the certainty that you are getting the husbands' prize produce, grown in their small country garden. Unfortunately, during my last visit to Ivrea, there were only a few of these vendors left; even in Italy, large-scale cultivation is replacing the small producer. To meet the increasing demand dictated by expanding supermarket power (which is bound by bureaucratic rules of European legislation), we are condemned to a very limited choice of vegetables, which also have to have certain narrow characteristics.

Our lazy shopping habits are also to blame – we are happy to buy beautiful-looking vegetables which are completely flavourless. Watching those poor vegetables, trapped in their plastic bags, really brings tears to my eyes. I am sorry to sound like such a romantic, but real pleasure lies in taking a carrot or potato from the soil in one's own garden and

enjoying it freshly boiled, without butter or anything else as its taste speaks for itself. There is some hope now because more and more farmers are growing vegetables organically, just as they used to.

The cooking of seasonally produced vegetables in Italy is continuous. The Italians' wonderful culinary imagination is applied to anything green and fresh, resulting in extremely tasty and healthy dishes as accompaniments to meat or fish, or for serving just by themselves. In fact, Italians don't divide food into vegetarian or non-vegetarian, because we love vegetables just as much as we do meat. When vegetables play the 'secondary role' of accompanying a main course, we prepare them to complement the main dish and provide an interesting combination. Italians love versatility in food and the average meal contains ingredients to achieve a natural balance of nutritionally essential items, like proteins, vitamins and fats.

All of this is, naturally, the result of centuries of development in the kitchens of rich and poor alike. The essential factor is to achieve something very tasty and wholesome – a family meal. Although one tends to think that rich people would eat special, expensive food, the modern way of viewing food is to adapt the very 'poor' ingredients cooked in the simple way of the poor. This is not snobbishness, but the desire to eat something very satisfying uncomplicated and tasty.

In this book you will find many recipes adopted from the so-called 'poor man's kitchen'. These have been developed over centuries from regional and local cuisine, along with influences from neighbouring countries. The dishes are usually very simple and can be adapted as a main course or a side dish. When my mother used to cook fried peppers, she always made sure she cooked more for me and my brothers to devour as a welcome snack with bread when we came home late. More than once, impromptu midnight feasts were held in front of our open fridge while we raided it and polished everything off! Stuffed peppers or aubergines were a complete meal in themselves.

Purposely try to leave some extra food in your fridge and you will see that magically by morning the fridge will be empty – especially if you have ravenous teenagers, but don't forget to hide some away for yourself!

Zuppa di Verdure
VEGETABLE SOUP

2 tbsp olive oil

1 onion, sliced

2 garlic cloves, chopped

12 cherry tomatoes

1 litre (1¾ pints) chicken or vegetable stock

150 g (5 oz) new potatoes, peeled and cut into slices 5 mm (¼ in) thick

2–3 courgettes, cut into slices 5mm (¼ in) thick

1 kg (2 lb 3 oz) tenerume (see below) or 2–3 more courgettes, chopped

salt and pepper

Heat the oil in a large pan, add the onion and garlic and fry briefly until softened. Add the tomatoes, stir well together, then pour in the stock and bring to a simmer. Add the potatoes, courgettes and tenerume, and cook for about 20 minutes or until the potatoes are tender.

Season to taste and then serve immediately with some good bread.

This soup uses *tenerume*, the tender shoots at the top of a courgette plant, including the young flower and courgettes still attached.

Courgette

To get the best courgettes, look for those which are firm to the touch with a shiny skin. Inside they should be white with small edible seeds. They are grown all over Italy and they adapt themselves quite readily to many soil types. They are universally popular for their culinary versatility and their nutritional value. Tenerume or tender courgette plant tops can be used at the end of the season to make a zuppa with potatoes, tomatoes, garlic and extra-virgin olive oil.

Courgette Flowers

*Like other plants in the squash family,
courgettes have exquisite flowers which are
edible. Only the non-fruit-bearing male
flower, with its characteristic long thin
stem, is usually sold in huge bunches at
markets all around Italy. Courgette flowers
are at their best when open and are ideal
for stuffing with mixtures of spinach,
ricotta and Parmesan before being dipped
in beaten egg and deep-fried. They are also
good simply dipped in a batter of flour,
water and salt then deep- or shallow-fried
in good olive oil.*

*Recently, due to demand for the flowers,
courgette plants have been bred expressly
for their flowers and only tiny courgettes are
produced as a result. These baby courgettes
are extremely tender but, like all plants
that are not allowed to reach maturity,
lack flavour in comparison with the fully
grown vegetable.*

Fiori di Zucchini Ripieni

STUFFED COURGETTE FLOWERS

12 courgette flowers
275 g (10 oz) ricotta cheese
pinch of freshly grated nutmeg
bunch of chives, chopped
1 egg, beaten
4 tbsp freshly grated Parmesan cheese
4 tbsp olive oil
salt and pepper
FOR THE BATTER:
2 eggs
55 g (1¾ oz) plain flour
4 tbsp cold water

First make the batter: beat the eggs lightly in a bowl, then stir in the flour evenly. Gradually add the water to make a smooth consistency. Set aside.

Clean the courgette flowers carefully. Gently wash and dry the outside and make sure there are no insects inside. Prepare the filling by mixing together the ricotta, nutmeg, chives, egg, grated Parmesan and some salt and pepper. Fill the flowers with spoonfuls of this mixture.

Heat the oil in a large frying pan. Dip the flowers in the batter and fry them, a few at a time, in the hot oil until golden brown, turning from time to time. Drain on paper towels before serving.

Carciofi in Agrodolce

SWEET-AND-SOUR ARTICHOKES

12 young and fresh medium artichokes
3 tbsp white wine vinegar
1 tbsp caster sugar
3 tbsp coarsely chopped flat-leaf parsley
3 tbsp extra-virgin olive oil
salt

Discard the tough outer leaves of the artichokes until you reach the tender leaves, then slice off the top. Trim the stems, leaving about 5 cm (2 inches) still attached; if you peel this it will be edible and very tender. Cut the artichokes into quarters and remove the choke with a knife. Boil the artichokes in lightly salted water for about 15 minutes or until tender; check by piercing with the tip of a knife. Drain and set aside.

Heat the vinegar and sugar in a small pan until the sugar has dissolved. Leave to cool, then mix with the parsley, olive oil and a pinch of salt. Pour over the artichoke quarters and leave to absorb the flavours for an hour or so before serving.

The sweetness is usually provided by sugar or honey and the sourness by vinegar or lemon juice, in combination with other flavourings like garlic, herbs and spices.

Globe Artichoke

Artichokes are full of protein, vitamins and fibre, as well as containing phosphorus, calcium, potassium, sodium, iron, copper and zinc. In Italy, they are eaten raw in salads or in pinzimonio *and* bagna caôda, *but they may also be blanched, quartered, dipped in flour and beaten egg and then deep-fried. They are also cooked in* umido *with tomatoes and olive oil. I like them slowly braised in plenty of extra-virgin olive oil, with onions, capers and parsley.*

One of the most delicious ways of cooking artichokes is as they do in Sicily. The leaves are loosened from the top with the fingers and coarse sea salt scattered over the centre. Extra-virgin olive oil is then sprinkled on top and the artichoke placed on a bed of charcoal embers and cooked slowly until the outer leaves are charred, but the heart is deliciously tender and with a smoky flavour.

Carciofi Ripieni
STUFFED ARTICHOKES

1 kg (2¼ lb) very fresh young artichokes

300 g (10½ oz) fresh breadcrumbs

small sprig of mint, roughly chopped

zest of ½ lemon

3 anchovy fillets, finely chopped

1 small garlic clove, very finely chopped

2 tbsp chopped flat-leaf parsley

25 g (¾ oz) salted capers, soaked in water for 10 minutes, then
   drained and roughly chopped

3 tbsp extra-virgin olive oil

salt and pepper

olive oil

Discard the tough outer leaves of the artichokes until you reach the tender leaves, then slice off the top. Cut off the stems so they will stand upright. Remove the choke from the centre with the help of a melon baller or sharp spoon, leaving a cavity.

Soak the breadcrumbs in a little water to cover, then squeeze out the excess moisture. Mix the breadcrumbs with the mint, lemon zest, anchovies, garlic, parsley and capers. Stir in the extra-virgin olive oil, then add a little salt and plenty of pepper.

Fill the cavity of the artichokes with this mixture and put the artichokes in a large pan, making sure they stay upright. Add enough water to come half way up the artichokes and then pour in enough olive oil to increase the level of the liquid by about 1 cm (½ inch). Bring to a simmer, cover with the lid and braise over a very gentle heat for 30 minutes.

Capers

The caper is a bud of a plant with very pretty thick round or oval-shaped leaves. The little islands of Lipari and Pantelleria, south of Sicily, produce capers of excellent quality. The smallest capers are the most sought after, because of their pungent flavour and tenderness. Like olives, capers are bitter and inedible when raw and need to be cured before being eaten. When you want to use them, soak them in water for about 15 minutes.

The best way to use capers is to add them to a dish, either chopped or whole, towards the end of the preparation, so that they keep their flavour and do not turn bitter. Capers can be used to flavour salads, tomato sauces, pasta or cooked vegetables like artichokes or broad beans. They can also be used to add piquancy to tuna fish sauces, as in vitello tonnato.

Frittata di Carciofi

ARTICHOKE OMELETTE

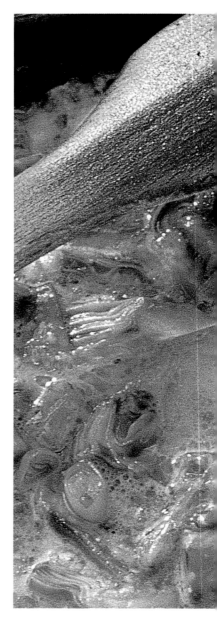

8 young and fresh medium artichokes
4 tbsp olive oil
1 large onion, thinly sliced
6 free-range eggs
2 tbsp coarsely chopped flat-leaf parsley
45 g (1½ oz) Parmesan cheese, grated
salt and pepper

Discard the tough outer leaves of the artichokes until you reach the tender leaves, then slice off the top. If the artichokes are young and tender, simply trim the stems, leaving about 5 cm (2 inches) still attached, then peel them. Cut them into quarters and remove the choke with a knife.

Put the artichokes in a frying pan with the olive oil, onion and about 6 tablespoons of water. Cover and cook gently until they are tender and all the liquid has evaporated.

Beat the eggs with the parsley, Parmesan cheese and some salt and pepper. Pour the egg mixture on to the artichokes and leave to set over a moderate heat without stirring. After a little while the eggs will have solidified and the frittata is ready. Serve cut into wedges.

Left: Frittata di Carciofi;
right: Carciofi in Agrodolce (page 15)

Asparagus

Asparagus needs to be prepared and cooked with special care and, to my mind, the best way to cook it is by steaming, so that the delicate tip stays intact after cooking and retains its flavour. To be eaten at its best, asparagus should be very fresh, the finest being those with firm heads with tightly closed tips. To prepare them, peel away the tough and stringy skin at the base. If you boil the asparagus, stand it in a tall, narrow pan, keeping the tender tips out of the water so that they do not overcook. Do not cover the pan with a lid, otherwise the heat of the steam cooks the tips faster than the stems.

In Italy, the most popular way of cooking asparagus is boiling it for serving with melted butter and a sprinkling of Parmesan cheese or perhaps, as they do it in Milan, with a fried egg on top. They are good pasticciati, that is mixed in chunks with onion and scrambled eggs. In spring-time, asparagus is delicious eaten with freshly boiled new potatoes, dressed with a little melted butter and accompanied with a few slices of thinly cut Parma ham.

Asparagi alla Emiliana
ASPARAGUS EMILIAN-STYLE

800 g (1¾ lb) green asparagus
100 g (3½ oz) Parmesan cheese, grated
85 g (3 oz) butter, melted
salt and pepper

Peel the lower stem of the asparagus, discarding all the stringy parts. Boil in lightly salted water until the stalks are just tender but still *al dente*, ensuring that the tips are intact.

Drain the asparagus, then arrange the spears all pointing in the same direction on serving plates and sprinkle over the Parmesan cheese. Season with salt and pepper to taste, then pour the hot melted butter over the tips and serve immediately.

This dish announces the arrival of summer. Asparagus is a wonderful vegetable which goes extremely well with dairy produce. I prefer the green to the white.

Risotto con Asparagi

ASPARAGUS RISOTTO

900 g (2 lb) fresh asparagus

about 1 litre (1¾ pints) vegetable stock

1 small onion, finely chopped

4 tbsp olive oil

85 g (3 oz) butter

350 g (12 oz) carnaroli or vialone nano rice

55 g (1¾ oz) Parmesan cheese, grated

salt and pepper

Trim the asparagus and cook it in boiling salted water until tender. Drain, reserving the cooking liquid. Cut the asparagus into 1-cm (½-inch) chunks, leaving the tips whole. Make up the asparagus cooking liquid with stock to 1.75 litres (3 pints) and keep at simmering point.

In a large, heavy-based pan, sweat the onion in the oil and half of the butter until soft, then add the chopped asparagus but not the tips. Stir in the rice until coated in the fat. Then add a ladleful of the stock and stir until it has been absorbed. Continue to add the stock in this way, stirring constantly, for about 15 minutes, until most of the stock has been used. Test a grain of rice and add more stock as necessary. The rice is done when tender on the outside but firm in the centre.

Remove from the heat and beat in the cheese and remaining butter. Season to taste. Decorate with the asparagus tips before serving.

Fields of risotto rice in Pizzarosto near Vercelli

Rice

The rice eaten by Italians is produced almost entirely in Italy. The variety cultivated by the Italians is ideally suited to making risotto, the most Italian of rice dishes. The main characteristic of risotto rice is that it is able to absorb moisture and swell by to up to three times its initial volume on being cooked, while still retaining a bite in its centre. In other words, it has to be al dente like pasta to makes it palatable.

The plant's Latin name is Oryza sativa. *It is planted in the spring and reaches maturity after about 140 to 180 days. During this time, great care must be taken to keep it steeped in water and to protect it from pests. The rice is harvested between September and October. It is then completely dried and the grains are sorted, washed and separated from their husks before being polished to a perfect white grain. The polishing is a very delicate operation because only the smallest amount of the surface of the grain should be removed to preserve nutrients. Ideally rice should be eaten whole, with the husk on, but this would impair its vital quality of absorbency.*

Pizzoccheri
BUCKWHEAT PASTA WITH POTATOES AND CABBAGE

Buckwheat Pasta

To make buckwheat pasta, mix together 250 g (9 oz) buckwheat flour and 100 g (3½ oz) 00 (doppio zero) flour, then pile them up into a volcano shape on a work surface. Make a well in the centre and add 2 eggs, 4 tbsp milk and a pinch of salt, plus enough water to make a fairly firm dough. Knead for 8–10 minutes, until smooth and elastic, then cover and leave to rest for 20 minutes. Roll out with a rolling pin to 5 mm (¼ inch) thick and cut into strips about 6 cm (2½ inches) long by 1 cm (½ inch) wide. Either use straight away or store in the refrigerator for up to 2 days.

350 g (12 oz) pizzoccheri (buckwheat pasta)
2 large potatoes, peeled and cut into small cubes
500 g (1 lb 1½ oz) Savoy cabbage, cut into strips
2 garlic cloves, sliced
6 sage leaves
100 g (3½ oz) butter
300 g (10½ oz) bitto, toma or asiago cheese, thinly sliced
85 g (3 oz) Parmesan cheese, grated
salt and pepper

If using freshly made pasta, cook the potatoes and cabbage in lightly salted boiling water until almost tender, then add the pizzoccheri for the last 6–8 minutes. If using dried pasta, cook everything together until tender.

Meanwhile, fry the garlic and sage very gently in the butter, then remove from the heat.

Drain the pizzoccheri and vegetables, arrange a layer of them in a preheated dish and cover with some of the cheese slices. Reheat the butter, garlic and sage until the butter is foaming. Pour a little of the hot butter and garlic over the cheese and sprinkle with some of the Parmesan cheese. Repeat these layers, then pour the remaining butter and garlic over the top. Leave for 1–2 minutes and then mix everything from top to bottom to check that the cheese has melted.

Spread the mixture on a warmed plate, season with salt and pepper and serve straight away.

Frittella Palermitana

ARTICHOKES, PEAS AND BROAD BEANS FROM PALERMO

4–5 small young artichokes

90 ml (3 fl oz) olive oil

1 large onion, thinly sliced

150 g (5 oz) shelled fresh peas

150 g (5 oz) shelled fresh broad beans

1 tsp salted capers, soaked in water for 10 minutes, then drained

2 tbsp chopped flat-leaf parsley

300 ml (½ pint) water

salt and pepper

Remove the stalks and tough outer leaves from the artichokes. Small young artichokes have hardly any choke and need very little preparation. Cut the artichokes into quarters, removing the choke if necessary.

Heat the oil in a saucepan, add the onion and fry briefly, until softened. Add the peas, broad beans, artichokes, capers, parsley and some salt and pepper, then pour in the water and stir well. Put the lid on the pan and cook over a moderate heat for about 20 minutes or until the vegetables are tender, stirring from time to time.

In Sicily they enjoy this dish when the vegetables are overcooked. However, I prefer it cooked my way so that the vegetables remain separate.

Broad Beans

When buying fresh broad beans, check that the pod is shiny and firm and that the beans inside are firm and tightly packed. One major tip when buying broad beans is to allow for the fact that three-quarters of the weight will have to be discarded, so if you need 500 g (1 lb) of shelled beans then you will need to buy 2 kg (4 lb).

I like broad beans cooked with onions and speck or Parma ham cut into little cubes. They are also good reduced to a purée and eaten with pork.

Panelle di Palermo
CHICKPEA FRITTERS

1 litre (1¾ pints) water
250 g (9 oz) chickpea flour
1 tbsp finely chopped flat-leaf parsley
salt and pepper
olive oil for frying

Bring the water almost to the boil in a large pan, then take off the heat and gradually add the chickpea flour, mixing very well in order to prevent lumps forming. When all the flour has been added, put the pan back on the heat and cook for about 30 minutes, stirring all the time. Add the parsley and season with salt. Pour the mixture on to a wet marble surface or baking sheet and flatten with a spatula to about 1 cm (½ in) thick.

When cool, cut into squares with a knife or into rounds with a pastry cutter. Shallow-fry in olive oil until golden brown on both sides.

Serve hot, with a sprinkling of freshly ground black pepper.

These are traditionally served with Frittella Palermitana (see page 29). Like many Sicilian dishes, it has a strong Arab influence.

Chickpeas

Popular all around the Mediterranean, this legume or pulse has been adopted by every Italian region, although it is cultivated only in the warmer South. It is probably the only legume that maintains a similar quality whether fresh or dry. Dried chickpeas need to be soaked in water for 8 to 24 hours, depending on their age. They can then be boiled for at least 3 hours. It is worth remembering that chickpeas double in volume and weight during cooking.

Dried chickpeas can also be ground to a flour and, in Italy, this is mainly used in Liguria to make farinata *or* faina, *a sort of flat bread.*

Panissa
BEANS AND RICE

300 g (10½ oz) dried borlotti beans
4 tbsp olive oil
1 large onion, finely sliced
100 g (3½ oz) pancetta, cut into small cubes
55 g (1¾ oz) Parma ham, cut into small cubes
400 g (14 oz) risotto rice such as carnaroli or arborio
100 ml (3½ fl oz) red wine, preferably nebbiolo or spanna
2 litres (3½ pints) chicken stock (from cubes is OK)
salt and pepper

Soak the beans in plenty of water overnight, then drain. Put them in a saucepan, cover with fresh water and simmer for about 2 hours or until tender. Drain.

Heat the olive oil in a pan, add the onion, pancetta and Parma ham and fry for 5–6 minutes. Add the rice and beans and stir well. Add the red wine and then continue as for making risotto (see page 23). Serve hot, without parmesan.
Serves 6

Ideally this should be made with fresh borlotti beans but because they are hard to come by outside Italy, you could use the dried ones.

Borlotti Beans

Borlotti are widely used in the famous northern Italian soup, pasta e fagioli, *which has become very popular all over Italy. In the North, however, it is prepared differently, in that half the beans are mashed to give a creamy and velvety texture to the soup. Borlotti are also good married with rice in the thick soup* panissa. *The Piedmontese town of Saluggia is also renowned for its borlotti dishes, which consist of borlotti bean soups cooked with cotenna (pork skin).*

Gattò di Patate
POTATO CAKE

1 kg (2¼ lb) floury potatoes

55 g (1¾ oz) prosciutto cotto, cut into cubes

25 g (¾ oz) buffalo mozzarella, cut into small cubes

100 g (3½ oz) provola cheese (smoked mozzarella), cut into small cubes

55 g (1¾ oz) Parmesan cheese, grated

4 eggs, beaten

2 tbsp finely chopped flat-leaf parsley

knob of butter

4 tbsp dried breadcrumbs

4 tbsp olive oil

salt and pepper

Potato

Of the many varieties of potato available,
the most important are the floury winter
potatoes such as Tonda di Napoli and
Bianca di Como, the white flesh of which is
used to make purées, gnocchi, croquettes
and toppings for savoury pies. They can
also be baked whole with their skins on, cut
into cubes or sliced with onions. They make
a useful thickener for soups such as
minestrone and a tasty accompaniment to
pasta in pasta e patate.

Preheat the oven to 180°C/350°F/gas 4. Boil the potatoes until tender, then drain and peel them. Pass them through a sieve to make a purée. Mix the potato purée with the prosciutto, mozzarella, provola, Parmesan, beaten eggs, parsley and some salt and pepper.

Use the butter to grease a round 25-cm (10-inch) cake tin, and dust with some of the breadcrumbs. Pour the potato mixture into it and press gently with a fork to give some shape. Sprinkle with the remaining breadcrumbs and then trickle over the olive oil. Bake for 30 minutes, until browned on top. Serve warm or cold.

Serves 6

The use of the term *gattò* (cake) dates back to the French occupation of Napoli.

Patate al Rosmarino

POTATOES WITH ROSEMARY

Rosemary

This evergreen herb grows in all the coastal regions of Italy and most families with a garden or balcony grow a small bush for their own use. The aromatic rosemary needles, with an underside of velvety grey, are carried on woody branches and the plant has an attractive blue flower in the summer.

The herb goes particularly well with any roasted meat. It can also be used, finely chopped, in marinades and in sauces, although it should be used carefully to avoid over-flavouring. If grilled over charcoal, rosemary gives a wonderful smoky flavour to meat and fish. It is best when used fresh as once dried the taste changes slightly.

1.5 kg (3¼ lb) waxy potatoes
a few sprigs of rosemary
4 sage leaves
abundant Tuscan extra-virgin olive oil for frying
salt

Peel the potatoes and boil them in lightly salted water for 10 minutes. Drain and cut into 2-cm (¾-inch) cubes.

Put a good layer of olive oil in a large frying pan over a medium heat and add the potatoes. Cook until tender and brown, stirring often to ensure that the potatoes brown on all sides. Add the rosemary and sage half way through cooking and season with salt just before serving.

Rosemary has such an intense flavour that it should be used carefully. Potatoes, however, can take strong flavours, especially when combined with peppery Tuscan olive oil.

Crocchette di Patate
MOZZARELLA-STUFFED POTATO CROQUETTES

800 g (1¾ lb) floury potatoes
4 tbsp freshly grated Parmesan cheese
3 egg yolks
1 tbsp finely chopped flat-leaf parsley
300 g (10½ oz) buffalo mozzarella, cut into fingers
1 egg white, lightly beaten
salt and pepper
dried breadcrumbs for coating
olive oil for deep-frying

Boil the potatoes in their skins until soft. Drain and peel while still warm. Pass them through a sieve to make a purée, then add the Parmesan cheese, egg yolks, parsley, and salt and pepper to taste. Mix well to give a fairly soft dough.

Cover the palm of your hand with the potato mixture. Put a mozzarella finger in the middle and cover it completely with more potato. Shape into a cylinder, making sure the mozzarella is in the centre. Repeat with the remaining potato mixture and mozzarella. Dip each croquette in the egg white, then roll in the breadcrumbs and deep-fry for a few minutes until crisp and brown. Serve warm.

Shopping for food, especially vegetables, is a major Italian pastime.

Capsicum

Although the pepper (peperone) should not to be confused with its close relative the peperoncino *or chilli pepper, it can still have a spiciness mingled with its sweet flavour. When cleaning it, discard the internal seeds and membranes and take care to wash your hands after handling them.*

As well as frying and preserving, peppers can also be grilled, skinned, cut into ribbons and dressed with olive oil, salt and garlic, before being served either hot or cold with all sorts of meat.

Peperoni al Pomodoro
PEPPERS AND TOMATOES

90 ml (3 fl oz) olive oil
600 g (1¼ lb) peperoncini dolci (see below), stems trimmed
1 garlic clove, finely chopped
400 g (14 oz) ripe tomatoes, peeled, deseeded and chopped (or the equivalent amount of polpa di pomodoro)
6 basil leaves
salt

Heat the oil in a pan and fry the whole peppers (the little seeds inside are edible) for 10 minutes, stirring constantly. Add the garlic and fry for a minute, then stir in the tomatoes, basil and salt. Cover and cook for about 15–20 minutes, until the peppers are soft.

My mother used to add some new potatoes and serve these as a first course accompanied by bread.

This is a common way of eating the very small peppers that look like chillies but taste sweet. When buying them you have to be sure to get the real thing.

Finocchio Fritto

FRIED FENNEL

3 large tender fennel bulbs
2 eggs, beaten
60 g (2 oz) butter
salt and pepper
flour for dusting

Cook the fennel bulbs in boiling salted water until tender; check
by inserting the tip of a knife. Drain and leave to cool, then cut into
quarters.

Beat the eggs with some salt and pepper. Dip the fennel segments
into the flour and then into the beaten egg to coat them completely.
Melt the butter in a pan over a gentle heat and fry the fennel until
golden on each side.

This is a very simple way to prepare fennel,
versatile enough to accompany all sorts of
delicate meat and fish dishes.

Bulb Fennel

*Fennel is used all over Italy, thinly sliced
in salads, baked in the oven with butter
and Parmesan cheese and blanched,
quartered, dipped in an egg batter and
deep-fried. One of the main signs of
summer for me is a fennel salad where
the bulb is thinly sliced then dressed with
extra-virgin olive oil, salt, pepper and a
few drops of lemon juice.*

Caponata

SICILIAN VEGETABLE STEW

1 large onion, chopped

3–4 celery stalks, including leaves, chopped

5 tbsp olive oil

1 kg (2¼ lb) aubergines, cut into 2.5-cm (1-in) chunks

1 tbsp salted capers, soaked in water for 10 minutes, then drained

20 green olives, stoned

1 tbsp sugar

1 tbsp white wine vinegar

55 g (1¾ oz) concentrated tomato paste

salt and pepper

Blanch the onion and celery in lightly salted boiling water for a few minutes, then drain.

Heat the oil in a large frying pan, add the aubergine chunks and fry until brown and tender (don't overcrowd the pan; you will probably have to cook them in batches). Add the onion, celery and all the remaining ingredients. Stir well, then cover and cook for about 15 minutes, removing the lid of the pan towards the end of cooking. Should the sauce require extra moisture, add a tablespoon or two of water during cooking. Season to taste with salt and pepper.

Serves 6

Aubergine

This vegetable is common throughout the Mediterranean region and used in an infinite number of recipes. In Italy, it is mainly eaten in the South and is grown in Campania, Puglia, Calabria, Sicily and Sardinia. Aubergines may be long and oval in shape or round like a huge egg. When fresh, they should be quite firm to the touch. They usually have rather tough skins, ranging in colour from dark purple to pale violet and even white (hence the American name eggplant). The pulp is white or slightly green, with a lot of little soft seeds. The aubergine has a slightly bitter taste, especially in the thinner varieties, so prior to cooking these are often sliced and sprinkled with salt, then left to rest while the bitter juices are drawn out.

Serve Caponata cold as an *antipasto*, warm as an accompaniment to meat or as a pasta sauce.

Mozzarella Caprese
MOZZARELLA, TOMATOES AND BASIL, CAPRI-STYLE

500 g (1 lb 1½ oz) buffalo mozzarella, sliced
2 large, ripe tomatoes, sliced
10 basil leaves
4 tbsp extra-virgin olive oil
salt and pepper

Arrange the slices of mozzarella on a plate, alternating them with the slices of tomatoes and basil leaves. Pour over a little stream of olive oil, then season with salt and pepper.

The best way of serving buffalo mozzarella as a starter is to combine it with ripe tomatoes, good olive oil and fresh basil. This is often called *insalata caprese*.

Mozzarella

*This southern Italian cheese is named after
the technique of tearing apart or cutting
(*mozzata*) the whey with the fingers to form
balls of cheese. It is mainly produced in
Battipaglia in the province of Salerno, but
is also made in Caserta and the provinces
of Naples, Puglia and Lazio. Authentic
buffalo-milk cheese is traditionally produced
by only a few specialists, as there is not
enough buffalo milk to meet the demands
of commercial production.*

*Fresh mozzarella has a sweet, nutty and
slightly salty flavour and is perfectly white.
It should also have a few holes inside,
where tears of whey seeped out when the
cheese was cut. In Lazio, especially around
Rome, another version of mozzarella,
called provatura, is made with a mixture of
whole cows' milk and pasteurized sheep's
milk. It is similar to the original cheese but
is harder in texture and with a yellowish
colour. A smoked version, called scamorza,
is produced in Campania, Abruzzo and
Molise. Mozzarella is delicious eaten
uncooked and sliced, dressed with a little
salt and pepper and a trickle of extra-virgin
olive oil.*

Insalata di Campo

WILD SALAD

Rocket

The longish but small, irregularly shaped leaves of ruchetta *have a sharp taste which is exceptionally good when mixed with other salad leaves. Rocket is often used as a tasty garnish for* carpaccio, *in a salad with tomatoes and mozzarella and as a flavouring for pasta sauces and sometimes risottos.* Rucola, *the cultivated version of* ruchetta, *has much larger and rounder leaves.*

300 g (10½ oz) trimmed weight of the following wild leaves, or any combination of them: dandelion, rocket, wild garlic, tender nettle leaves, lamb's lettuce or whatever you fancy
small bunch of spring onions
4 tbsp extra-virgin olive oil
30 g (1 oz) anchovy fillets, reduced to a pulp
1 garlic clove, very finely chopped
2 tbsp balsamic vinegar
salt and pepper

Thoroughly wash all the leaves and pat or spin them dry. Chop the spring onions into small chunks and arrange on a serving dish mixed with the leaves.

Put the oil, anchovies, garlic and balsamic vinegar in a small bowl with salt and pepper to taste. Mix well and pour over the salad. Toss to mix again and serve.

A popular springtime activity for many Italians is roaming the fields to collect the first tender leaves of the dandelion and other herbs for a hearty salad.

Cicoria Belga al Tartufo Nero

CHICORY WITH BLACK TRUFFLE

5 large heads of chicory or radicchio

1 tbsp truffle oil

2 tbsp extra-virgin olive oil

1 tbsp balsamic vinegar

1 summer truffle (Tuber aestiuum), weighing about 55 g (1¾ oz), thinly sliced

salt and pepper

Cut the chicory into strips 1 cm (½ inch) wide, removing the tough core which is slightly bitter. Put the chicory into a bowl and add the oils, vinegar, salt and pepper. Mix well and serve topped with thin slices of summer truffle.

This is one of the favourite starters in my restaurant. The simple combination produces an outstanding result. As they are closely related, it works just as well with radicchio as chicory.

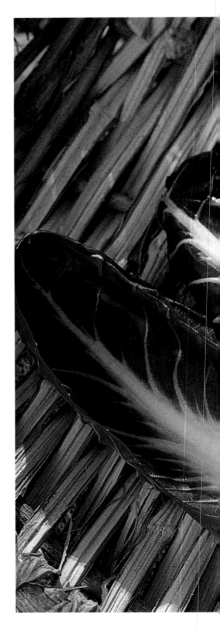

Giardiniera
MIXED GARDEN PICKLE

2 kg (4½ lb) mixed vegetables such as pickling onions, gherkins,
    cauliflower, carrots, celeriac and pumpkin
2 litres (3½ pints) white wine vinegar
1 litre (1¾ pints) water
55 g (1¾ oz) salt
30 g (1 oz) sugar
small handful of bay leaves
small handful of cloves
chilli, to taste (optional)
a few juniper berries (optional)

Peel the vegetables as necessary, then cut them into bite-sized chunks. Put the vinegar and water in a large pan with the salt and sugar and bring to the boil, stirring to dissolve the salt and sugar. Add the vegetables and simmer for 30 minutes, until tender.

Transfer the hot pickle to a 2.5-litre (4½-pint) sterilized preserving jar (or several smaller jars), tucking in the bay leaves, cloves, and chilli and juniper berries, if using. Seal the jar and store in a cool place. The pickle can be used straight away.

All over Italy *antipasto* is always served with some sort of pickle.

Cauliflower

Italian cuisine makes good use of the cauliflower in a range of dishes from minestrone to the famous regional dish of pasta e cavolfiore *from Campania. It is also wonderful puréed with butter and Parmesan cheese, served in a cheese sauce, au gratin (or gratinato, as the Italians say), made into simple salads cut into thin slices and dressed with oil and vinegar or dipped into mayonnaise, and freshly boiled and dressed with extra-virgin olive oil, garlic and lemon juice.*

Insalata di Rinforzo

REINFORCED SALAD

1 cauliflower
150 g (5 oz) black olives
200 g (7 oz) pickled yellow or red peppers
200 g (7 oz) Giardiniera (see page 52)
30 g (1 oz) large salted capers, soaked in
    water for 10 minutes, then drained
100 g (3½ oz) anchovy fillets
virgin olive oil, for sprinkling
finely chopped chilli (optional)

Cut the cauliflower into florets and cook in lightly salted boiling water until *al dente*, then drain. Put the cauliflower, olives, pickled peppers, *giardiniera* and capers in a bowl and sprinkle with olive oil, then transfer to a large screw-top jar. Decorate with a lattice of anchovy fillets, then seal the jar and store in a cool place. The salad should last throughout the festivities.

A typical Neapolitan dish made at the beginning of the Christmas season, this is called *rinforzo* (reinforcement) because it is topped up with fresh ingredients each time any is used to last throughout the festivities.

Glossary of Vegetables and Salads

Acetosa / *Sorrel*
This sharp-tasting plant, also known as *erba brusca* or 'sour grass', is not widely cultivated in Italy, although it can be found growing wild in May and June. It is used in soups and salads for its pungent flavour and I find it irresistible as a base for risotto.

Aglio, Aglietto / *Garlic*
Garlic has been cultivated in Italy for centuries and 70 per cent of its entire production is exported.

There are many varieties, including the white Bianco Napoletano and Bianco Piacentino, and the pink Rosso Napoletano, Rosso di Sulmona and Rosso di Agrigento. Sometimes in spring you can find *aglio selvatico* or wild garlic, but instead of eating the bulb eat only the dark-green scented leaves.

Remember that, when it comes to choosing garlic, small is beautiful. To spot a good-quality garlic bulb, look for one with compact, firm cloves. Avoid any with green shoots sprouting from the top as these are past their best.

If carefully trimmed and kept whole, garlic will keep for up to a year. To peel it, press on each clove with the palm of your hand until the skin breaks and comes away easily. If you want to get rid of the smell of garlic on your hands, rub them with salt before washing.

Asparago / *Asparagus*
Much loved by Italians, asparagus is generally only eaten in season so that its natural wild flavour can be enjoyed. Asparagus is a shoot which, if allowed to grow to maturity, blooms into a wonderful delicate lace-like head. When the tip emerges from the earth, it is cut at its base with a special long knife, leaving about 15 cm (6 inches) of tender edible shoot attached.

There are three main types of asparagus grown and enjoyed in Italy, the white, the purple and the green. The white variety, Bianco di Bassano, is derived from the German tradition and grows in the Veneto. Purple asparagus is called *argenteuil* and is cultivated in Campania, from which it also takes its Italian name of Napoletano, while the green variety is grown in Piedmont and Emilia-Romagna.

Barbabietola / *Beetroot*
This root is from the same family as sugar beet and is much loved as a cooked (or sometimes raw) root for salads. It is also the principal ingredient of soups like *borscht*.

Barba di Becco, Barba di Frate, Barba di Cappuccino / *Salad Green*
This salad plant is similar to chives and, like the herb, has long, narrow green leaves with a slightly sour taste. It is hardly cultivated, but grows wild all over Italy.

Borlotto / *Borlotti Bean*
One of the best-known and most popular beans in central and northern Italy, whether in its fresh or dried form the borlotti bean distinguishes itself from others by the startling patterns formed by its green and white skin colours. The pod (*baccello*) of the fresh bean is yellowish in colour, with bright red and green speckles while the bean itself is white with red speckles. It is harvested when the pods are completely dry and the beans have taken on a darker colour. It is mostly used in its dry form.

Borragine, Borrana / *Borage*
This robust flowering herb always makes me think of Liguria, where it is widely used in *preboggion*, a mixture of wild herbs, and it is also used in Campania to make a delicious soup. With its large hair-covered leaves, borage is better cooked and eaten as a fresh vegetable.

Broccolo, Broccoletto / *Broccoli, Calabrese*
Broccoli belongs to the same family as cabbage and comes in many different varieties. It is formed by thousands of buds at the top of the

plant. If the buds flower the broccoli becomes yellow and that is why its freshness is measured by the tightness and the intensity of the deep green-blue colour of the buds.

Broccolo is mostly known as calabrese, because it grows best in Calabria, and in Sicily (where, incidentally, broccolo means cauliflower). The most common variety, Piccolo di Verona, is pale green and ready for eating in the early spring, while Grosso Romano, or Violetto di Sicilia as it is also known in Italy, has very pretty conical florets and a distinctive purple colour that turns green during cooking.

Broccoletti are little branches of broccoli. Like Brussels sprouts, they grow on the main stem after the main flower has been cut off.

Broccolo di Rapa / *Turnip Shoot*
The little shoots of turnip look like little spears with flowerheads that turn yellow when they open. The shoots should only be used, however, while still green. *Broccolo di rapa* are very popular in the south, where they are called *friarielli*. They can be blanched before cooking to moderate their strong flavour.

Bruscandoli, Bruscansi / *Hop Shoot*
The hop is a climbing plant with small thorns and only the tops of tender young shoots are used in cooking. This plant grows wild all over Italy, but is a speciality of the Veneto, where it is used in risottos.

Cannellino / *Cannellini Bean*
A favourite with all Italians, especially in central Italy, cannellini beans have spread from the kitchens of Tuscany all over Italy. The popularity of the bean is due to its flavour, perfect creamy-white colour and ease of use in the kitchen.

The beans are difficult to harvest when ripe and are thus harvested in autumn, when the pod is completely dry. As a result, they are rarely eaten fresh.

Carciofo / *Globe Artichoke*
Artichokes belong to the thistle family. The edible parts of the plant are the tender parts of the flower bud and the adjacent stalk. They grow best in the Mediterranean region, where the climate and the well-drained soil are perfect. The major areas of production in Italy are Campania, Sicily, Puglia and Lazio, but they are grown in most regions.

Artichokes come in a wide variety of colours, from purple to green, as well as in a range of shapes – both with and without thorns. There are basically three sizes: the biggest and first to appear is *La Mamma*, which is usually boiled and eaten leaf by leaf until the fleshy heart is reached, with the hairy choke being discarded. Secondary, smaller plants, called *figli* (children) grow later just below the main head and are wonderfully tender. Finally, even smaller artichokes, called *nipoti* (nephews) grow

further down the plant and these are usually pickled for *antipasto*.

The main varieties are the Romanesco, a large purple globe artichoke without thorns. A smaller, very tender artichoke, the Violetto Toscano, is also purple in colour and, as its name implies, is cultivated in Tuscany. A violet artichoke from Sicily called Spinoso di Palermo has a fantastic flavour.

Cardo / *Cardoon*
The cardoon is related to the thistle and – like its other close relative, the artichoke – it has long leaves. Unlike the artichoke, however, it is the stem of the cardoon and not the flower that is eaten. To make it tender enough to eat, the cardoon is specially cultivated, as in Piedmont, where from around September to October the long stems and leaves are bent over (each region bends the stem in a different way) and covered with earth to protect them from the harsh winter weather. Over the following months they become perfectly white and extremely tender. Because of this peculiar way of blanching them they take on a curved shape and are commonly called *gobbi* (hunchbacks).

Carota, Pastinaca, Pastanache / *Carrot*
This root vegetable is available all year round and grows mostly in temperate climates, with Sicily and Abruzzo being the main areas of production in Italy. The carrot

ranges in colour from pale yellow to deep purple and has a strong aroma and taste.

Cavolfiore / *Cauliflower*
There are many varieties of *palla di neve* (snowball), the technical name given to this king of the cabbage family. In principle, it is the same as broccoli, except that the white florets which make up the head are extremely compact and heavy and surrounded by a few leaves whose freshness indicates the quality. The most tender of the leaves are edible. Cauliflowers are grown all over Italy, especially in Campania, Marche, Puglia and Sicily.

Cavolino di Bruxelles / *Brussels Sprout*
This sprout, which takes the form of a kind of mini cabbage, has only recently been adopted in Italy, despite the fact that Romans are said to have taken them to Belgium in the first place. The sprouts grow on the long stems of this member of the cabbage family up to 1 metre (1 yard) in height. They are harvested in late autumn through to winter.

Cavolo / *Cabbage*
This underrated vegetable is one of the foundations of modern Italian cuisine and is as popular in the South as the North. There are four basic types cultivated, with the precious summer variety grown in the North and the autumn and winter varieties in the warmer South.

Cavolo cappuccio (flat cabbage) has greeny-blue leaves on the outside and very white leaves on the inside. These internal leaves are very tender and are used to make crauti, the Italian equivalent of sauerkraut.

Cavola verza (Savoy cabbage) is distinguished from the other varieties by its wrinkled, curly leaves.

Cavolo nero (black cabbage) is an unusual variety, not just because the leaves are dark green, almost black, but because they are quite long and curled. It is mostly cultivated in the South and in Tuscany, where it forms part of the famous *ribollita* soup.

Cavolo cappuccio rosso (red cabbage) is deep red with leaves that grow so tightly together a cabbage can weigh around 1½ kg (3 lb).

Cavolo Rapa / *Kohlrabi*
Although this vegetable belongs to the cabbage family, it is the root and not the leaves that are eaten. The root can grow as large as a grapefruit, while its spindly stalks and leaves emerge from the top in a rather haphazard manner. It has a pale green skin and even paler flesh. When young it is extremely tender, with only a hint of cabbage flavour. Peel and discard the tough, woody skin before cooking.

Cetriolo, Cetriolini / *Cucumber, Gherkins*
The Italian cucumber is shorter than its English counterpart, as Italians prefer varieties like Marketer or Carosello which are not cylindrical but rounder, like their squash relatives. Great care has to be taken when choosing cucumbers; they should not be too big and should be quite hard to the touch. Peeling off the skin makes it more digestible, as does removing the seeds of larger varieties.

Cicerchia / *Pulse*
This type of dried bean, closely resembling the chickpea in both appearance and flavour, is widely used throughout Italy.

Cicoria, Cicorietta, Catalogna / *Chicory*
A great variety of different salad and vegetable plants belong under this name. Their common characteristic is that they are all bitter because they descend from the wild plant *Cicoria selvatica*, a close relation of the *dente di leone* (dandelion).

Catalogna is a cultivated relative of wild chicory, which is similar in shape to the dandelion but is much larger, growing up to 50 cm (1⅔ ft) high. Its dense leaves grow from a root which, along with the tender white part of the stems, can be braised in a similar way to the wild dandelion. *Catalogna puntarelle* (little tips) is a bushy variety of the same plant, with 20–30 tender, juicy little shoots attached to the root. *Cicoria di Bruxelles* (chicory or Belgian endive) has tightly packed creamy white leaves.

Radicchio is a salad leaf belonging to the chicory family that is widely used for its slightly bitter taste and its deep red-mauve colour. There are two principal varieties: Rossa di Verona, a round and tightly formed ball of leaves, similar to a small red cabbage and the famous Radicchio di Treviso, so called because it is mainly cultivated in that province. While Rossa di Verona is available all the year round, treviso only makes its appearance in winter, where it ripens from a reddish-green colour to a wonderful deep red. It is usually sold with the edible fleshy root attached.

Ceriolo verde and *ceriolo rosso* are two pretty salad leaves from the chicory family. They are both formed like a rose, one with green leaves and the other with red. Both have the typically bitter chicory taste. *Cicorietta da taglio* is another, quite tiny, salad leaf. The little plants are tightly sown so that they form a delicate green carpet and are cut at the base so that only the small tender leaves are used. It then grows back after being cut.

Scarola (Batavia) grows in the form of a bushy head of deep green with robust outer leaves, but only the pale cream and yellow centre is used in salads because the outer leaves are a little tough. *Indivia* (curly endive or frisée) is a curious salad leaf which is from the same branch of the family as scarola and is very similar, having tough outer leaves and a very tender centre.

Cime di Rapa / *Turnip Tops*
Also called *broccoletti di rapa*, this is the leafy top of the turnip. The leaves are used in much the same way as broccoli. The taste is stronger than broccoli and slightly bitter, and is much loved by the Romans and Neapolitans, who call them *friarielli*.

Cipolla, Cipollotto, Cipolline / *Onion*
The onion has been cultivated through the centuries to produce thousands of varieties.

The pink-and-golden-coloured onions have the most intense flavour, while the white and red are usually milder. The best red onions are those from Tropea in Calabria, celebrated for their sweetness.

Coste / *Swiss Chard*
Similar in flavour to spinach, chard is called *erbette* in Emilia-Romagna – the name used to refer to parsley in Rome. As well as cooking the leaves in the same way as spinach, the white ribs can be cut in chunks and braised until tender.

Dente di Leone / *Dandelion*
Also known as *pissialetto* because of their diuretic quality, wild dandelion leaves can be used in salad in spring, when they are very tender.

Fagiolino / *Green Bean*
This much appreciated vegetable comes in a widely varying number of varieties. Most green beans are collected when not quite mature, so that they are tender and full of flavour. The smallest and most slender is Contender, although the slightly larger Bobis (Italian for Bobby) has a little more substance and, when fresh and picked very young, in my opinion tastes much better. Re dei bleu, (King of the Blues) is much longer than either of these and has a good flavour.

Two other varieties of *fagiolini* are a creamy white colour rather than green. Burro di Roquencourt, Meraviglia di Venezia or Venice Wonder, a fairly large but very tender bean if picked young. An exceptionally long bean is the Stringa (string bean) which can reach up to 50 cm (20 inches) and is greeny-red.

Only the youngest, freshest beans do not need topping and tailing. To check the freshness of a bean, break it in half. If it snaps easily and is moist on the inside it is fresh.

Fava / *Broad Bean*
Broad bean plants grow up to a metre high, first producing a wonderfully white flower and then the fruit – the pod with the beans inside. Broad beans are a very old food indeed, taken up by the Romans after they were introduced to them by the Egyptians. For a long time they were the only beans eaten in Italy, and then mostly by peasants. Now the broad bean is cultivated with much enthusiasm all over Italy, although the main area of growth is in the warmer South.

Finocchio / *Bulb Fennel*
Fennel has such a sweet taste and pleasant aroma that it was often served at the end of a meal as a dessert in Italy. It is delicious in every form, raw or cooked. Fennel grows from spring through to October, depending on the area in which it is grown and which of the many varieties is cultivated.

Lampascione, Lampagione, Lampasciuolo / *Muscari*
This bulb of the *muscari* or wild hyacinth plant is much used in Puglia and southern Italy and is now cultivated to meet growing demand. Looking like a shallot, it is slightly bitter and is mostly eaten when it ripens in the summer.

Lattuga / *Lettuce*
The Italians are very fond of lettuce. A salad almost invariably contains one or two of the very different varieties grown in all seasons all over Italy. *Romana*, or *Cos*, is the most universally popular for its crispness and flavour. There is also *lattuga d'inverno* or winter lettuce, which is more resistant to cold weather, and *insalata primaverile* (springtime lettuce), with its pale but very tender leaves.

Lenticchia / *Lentil*
The lentil comes from a small climbing plant never growing more than 50 cm (20 inches) high. Its rectangular pods usually contain 4 lentils each. The name lentil comes

from the Latin lens, which incidentally gave the name to the optical lens as it has a similar shape.

There are various varieties of lentils, all bearing the name of the area where they are produced. The best-known are the *lenticchie di castelluccio* from Umbria, which are organically grown, very tasty, full of iron and many vitamins.

Misticanza, Mesticanza / *Wild Salad*
This is a Roman expression for a mixture of wild salad leaves, including mint, rocket, dandelion, garlic, fennel and sorrel, usually mixed with traditional greens like endive or lettuce. The same word in Umbria means a mixture of dried beans to make soup.

Ortica / *Nettle*
One of the most annoying of weeds, nettles are nevertheless edible and enjoyable. There are various types, but the edible one is the common stinging nettle with a greenish-white flower. It is essential that you wear gloves when you pick the tender spring tips. To stop them from stinging, put them in the refrigerator for a while, then boil them for 5 minutes or until tender.

Pannocchia / *Corn on the Cob*
Grilled tender young corn cobs are called *pannocchia di granoturco arrostita* and boiled corn on the cob

pannocchia lessa. In season these are sold at little stands by the roadside, especially in the South.

Patata / *Potato*
Although fulfilling the same role in northern Europe as bread in southern Europe, the potato has never been part of the staple diet in Italy. Indeed it was only in the middle of the nineteenth century that it started to be widely used as a vegetable in Italy. Originally from South America, the potato is mostly cultivated in the Veneto, Puglia, Campania and Calabria, where the soil is particularly well suited to it.

Peperone / *Capsicum*
Along with the aubergine, the sweet pepper is perhaps the vegetable most closely associated with Mediterranean countries. Native to South America, it was introduced to Italy towards the end of the eighteenth century, when it became a popular ingredient. The cultivation of the pepper, which takes its name from its spicy flavour similar to that of a peppercorn, is widespread throughout Italy.

The squarish Quadrato di Asti is grown all over Italy, but most notably near Carmagnola in Piedmont. Of the other varieties, there is the Carnoso di Cuneo, a large meaty pepper of yellow or red and sometimes green. Another variety looks like a tomato, being bright red in colour and square-looking, almost squashed. Peppers may also be long and conical, like the lungo Marconi. I think the best peppers are the yellow and red, but the very small green ones are good cooked whole, although it is worth tasting one first to check the flavour. These are called *puparuoli* in Naples.

Pisello / *Pea*
Peas are grown in almost every region in Italy as the plant can grow in most climates. The best-known varieties are Senatore, Superbo di Luxton, Piccolo Provenzale and Meraviglia d'Italia. When buying peas, the pod should be as fresh a green as the pea itself. If it is yellow or a pale green it means that the peas are old and will be hard. Try to insist on being able to open and sample at least one pod.

Also a member of the pea family is the *taccola* or *pisello mangiatutto* (mange-tout pea), where the pod and the barely developed pea inside are eaten as one.

Pomodoro / *Tomato*
This vegetable fruit is one of the most versatile and important of foods, and forms the backbone of much of Italian cooking.

Originally from Mexico, the tomato was brought back by explorers and made its first appearance in Europe in the second half of the 16th century. For a long time it was considered to be a curiosity, used more as an ornament rather than in the kitchen. In Italy, the first appearance of the tomato in cooking was

recorded in a book by Vincenzo Corrado in 1765, *Cuoco Galante* (The Gallant Cook). From that moment on, the tomato was taken to the Italian heart.

Once it was discovered which regions had the best climate and soil, the tomato became – alongside pasta – among the first industrialized food products to be used all year round. All Italians who had access to a little land cultivated and produced tomatoes for themselves, which they consumed either raw or preserved in bottles. Among the most famous varieties of tomatoes to be eaten raw in salads are Cuor di Bue (Ox's heart) and Palla di Fuoco (Fireball). In southern Italy they prefer to eat tomatoes very ripe and they also eat a variety of tomato which is usually used in preserving, the San Marzano. In the North, they prefer the tomato to be almost green with a lot of acidity. They use these in salads, not using any vinegar for dressing, just virgin olive oil, salt and pepper.

The San Marzano, Roma, Napoli and Marena are all types of tomatoes preferring a rich potash soil – like the wonderful terrain around the Vesuvius area where material from the volcano has made the soil extremely fertile. These varieties are mostly used for canning or bottling. These are the bright-red plum-shaped tomatoes that you can find in cans worldwide, not requiring the addition of sugar to make sauces.

The *pomodorino* (cherry tomato or vine tomato) is small and grows

in bunches. This type of tomato is mostly found in the South, Puglia, Sicily and Calabria and generally used fresh. It has a tough skin, does not grow bigger than a cherry and can be kept in bunches for the entire winter. It is consumed raw in salads, but is mainly used in the preparation of quick pasta sauces. Of the varieties grown, the *pomodorino di Cerignola* is the most sought-after.

Porro / *Leek*
This vegetable is like a cross between garlic and onion – and belongs to same family. It is cultivated all over Italy, but mainly in Liguria, Marche, Abruzzo and Puglia. The Romans took this vegetable with them all over Europe. Those cultivated in the summer are more tender and they are usually eaten raw.

Portulaca / *Purslane*
This wild leafy summer plant grows almost anywhere and is characterized by its reddish branches which spread over the ground. It has small thick leaves which, when young, add a special juiciness to salads.

Rapa / *Turnip*
Belonging to the cabbage family, the turnip is one of the most widely used winter vegetables. It has a delicate flavour akin to that of kohlrabi. Turnips need to be thoroughly cleaned and as little of the skin as possible removed. Raw, very young turnips can be shredded into salads.

Ravanello / Radish
This wonderful vegetable is mainly eaten raw. The little roots come in varying shapes, from round or conical to straight. They are very hot in flavour, but refreshing, and their red and white colouring can enliven many salads and *antipasto* plates.

Scalogno / Shallot
The shallot, which looks like a small onion, is divided into two sections inside. Its flavour falls somewhere between the onion and garlic, but its use is limited to flavouring sauces cooked with butter and scattering raw and finely chopped on salads. Shallots keep better than onions, and so can be stored for a long time.

Scorzonera / Black Salsify
This very long, straight root vegetable belongs to the lettuce family. Harvested in autumn and winter it is enjoyed for its delicate but bitter flavour. The root can grow up to 30 cm (1 foot) long and must be thoroughly scraped with a knife until the white pulp is visible. If it is old, cut it in two and discard the woody centre. If it is very young, though, it can be boiled whole and eaten with melted butter like asparagus.

Sedano, Sedano Rapa / Celery, Celeriac
Celery is valuable both as a herb and as a vegetable. There are two basic varieties. One is a plant with a long stem of deep green on the outside and creamy white on the inside. The other is sedano rapa (turnip-rooted celery or celeriac) which grows mainly underground in a round root. The leaves are sold as a herb for salads and soups. They have a strong scent and their skins are quite tough but full of flavour.

Celery is grown almost everywhere in Italy but most notably in Puglia, Calabria and Campania.

Spinaci / Spinach
The Arabs introduced this popular vegetable to Italy around the year AD 1000 and it is now grown in northern and central Italy, where the climate is mild but not hot. It grows close to the ground and has substantial deep green leaves.

Valerianella / Lamb's Lettuce
One of the most delicate wild salad leaves, this plant is now widely cultivated. It is used largely in modern cuisine to decorate various dishes and is usually eaten raw on its own or as part of a green salad. The little bushy leaves are extremely tender and delicate.

Zucca / Squash, Pumpkin
One of the most widely used family of vegetables in Italy, all types of squash, pumpkins and the smaller courgettes (see right) are loved for their flavour, varying shapes, and wide range of uses in the kitchen. Only the marrow is not much eaten in Italy, as it is considered to be no more than an overgrown courgette but without the flavour.

Pumpkin and other thick-skinned winter squashes will keep for up to a month as long as the skin is not broken. Once cut, however, they will only last for a day or two. For the best flavour, they should only be picked when fully ripe.

One unusual variety of squash is the spaghetti pumpkin, whose cooked flesh resembles strings, like spaghetti. It is delicious eaten simply with butter and Parmesan.

Squash and pumpkin flowers are used in the same way as courgette flowers. Generally slightly smaller than those of the courgette, they do however have a more intense flavour.

Zucchino / Courgette
Like the other larger zucca, zucchini grow over the ground but are more bushy than other plants in the family. When buying them, try to get organically grown ones and try to buy them in season when their flavour is at its best. Courgettes come in a huge range of shapes, colours and sizes, from the round, dark green Tonda di Nizza to the long, straight dark green Verde di Milano and from the common Striata di Italia or di Napoli to the pale green Bianca Sarda. What they all have in common though, is their flavour, which is almost exactly the same regardless of their appearance.

Index

Publishing Director: Anne Furniss
Creative Director: Mary Evans
Editor: Lewis Esson
Consultant Art Director: Helen Lewis
Design: Sue Storey
Assistant Editor: Jane Middleton
Editorial Assistant: Rhian Bromage
Production: Candida Jackson &
   Vincent Smith

This edition published in 1999 by
Quadrille Publishing Limited,
Alhambra House,
27-31 Charing Cross Road,
London WC2H OLS

Based on material originally published
in *Carluccio's Complete Italian Food*.

Text © 1997 & 1999 Carluccio's Partnership
Photography © 1997 André Martin
Design, edited text and layout © 1999
Quadrille Publishing Ltd

The rights of the authors have been
asserted.

Cataloguing-in-Publication Data:
a catalogue record for this book is
available from the British Library.

ISBN 1 899988 49 1

Printed and bound in Hong Kong.